Addiction

The "High" That Brings You Down

DISCARD

Miriam Smith McLaughlin
and
Sandra Peyser Hazouri

Enslow Publishers, Inc.

44 Fadem Road   PO Box 38
Box 699   Aldershot
Springfield, NJ 07081 Hants GU12 6BP
USA   UK

Library of Congress Cataloging-in-Publication Data

McLaughlin, Miriam Smith.
    Addiction: the "high" that brings you down / Miriam Smith McLaughlin, Sandra
Peyser Hazouri.
        p.cm. — (Teen issues)
    Includes bibliographical references and index.
    Summary: Discusses the problems associated with a family member,
parent or child, who suffers from addiction.
    ISBN 0-89490-915-0
    1. Teenagers—Drug use—United States—Juvenile literature, 2. Drug abuse—
United States—Juvenile literature. 3. Narcotic addicts—United States—Family
relationships—Juvenile literature. 4. Children—Drug use—United States—Juvenile
literature. [1. Drug abuse.] I. Hazouri, Sandy. II. Title. III. Series.
HV5824.Y68M424 1997
362.2'9—dc20   96-32675
                                                      CIP
                                                      AC

Printed in the United States of America

10 9 8 7 6 5 4 3 2

Cover Illustration: © C/B PRODUCTIONS

Contents

Authors' Note

The stories included in this book are true, but names and circumstances have been changed to protect confidentiality.

Special thanks to the counselors and students who so willingly shared their experiences for this book.

True or False

What Do You Know About Addiction?

Read the following statements and decide if they are true or false. On a piece of paper or in a notebook write a column of numbers from 1 to 12. Write T or F for each statement on your own paper. Do not write in this book.

1. The addict is only hurting himself or herself.
2. It is easy to identify families that are dealing with addiction problems.
3. Very few schoolchildren have an addicted parent.
4. Healthy families have arguments.

5. Children can cause a parent's addiction to get worse.
6. Children of addicts may be at risk of being addicted themselves.
7. Some people are addicted to behaviors like gambling and eating.
8. Teenagers from families in which someone is an addict may have difficulty having healthy relationships.

9. Not everyone who drinks is an alcoholic.
10. Addicted teenagers are less mature than their peers.
11. A support group is made up of people who have had similar life experiences and who help each other understand and cope with their problems.
12. Alateen is for young people from families in which there is alcoholism.

Answers on Page 101

1

Healthy Families/ Addicts' Families

Melissa, who is eighteen, lives in a family in which there is alcohol addiction. Her parents are among the millions of Americans who are addicted to something; alcohol, food, gambling, and drugs are common addictions. She is one of the many young people in our country growing up in a home where addiction is holding the family hostage. For Melissa, her home life is traumatic.

> The screaming frightened me. The more they drank, the louder they got. One night they were throwing dishes at each other. It reminded me of the war sounds I've heard on television. I locked the door to my room, sat on the bed, and tried to read my assignment for English. Finally, I heard my father yell, "I'm outta here!" Then the front door slammed and it was completely silent.

The addict uses all available resources to support his or her addiction. The family must spend all its energy trying to survive the effects of the addict's behavior. Young people like Melissa often do not get their needs met in these families and may grow up feeling unloved, worthless, angry, and afraid. As a society, we have always recognized the problems of the addicted person. Only in recent years have we come to understand the damaging effects of the addiction on the people who live with the addict.

What is Addiction?

The notion of what addiction is varies according to the group of experts defining it and the addiction they are trying to characterize. Addictions to drugs and alcohol are by far the most common and most researched compulsions; however, addictions to particular activities and behaviors can be equally destructive. For the purposes of this book, we will define *addiction* as the overwhelming urge to use a substance or do an activity, regardless of the consequences. This definition describes both substance abuse and behavior addictions.

The Physiological Theory. There are several theories that help to define addiction further. The physiological theory applies most readily to drug and alcohol addiction, because it identifies the impact of the use of a substance on the physical body. This model views addiction as resulting from some biochemical, metabolic, or genetic disorder.[1] Drug and alcohol abuse cause major changes in brain chemistry that are very difficult to reverse. There is also extensive research to support the existence of genetic factors that influence alcoholism.

The Disease Model. This theory views addiction as primary, chronic, and progressive, with a predictable outcome if it is not treated. In this model, addiction is comparable to high blood pressure or diabetes. Addiction is primary because it is not a symptom of some other disorder. It is chronic because the affected person will always have the disease. It is progressive because the disease of addiction gets worse over time if it is not treated and, if it is left untreated, it leads to death.[2] Although the disease model originated as a way of defining alcoholism, it is now applied to drug and behavioral addictions like gambling and eating.

The Social Learning Model. The third theory looks at all addictions, including alcohol and drug addictions, as behaviors that develop in the same way that all other behaviors develop. The addict, according to this theory, learned to use a substance or do an activity in order to relieve pain or promote good feelings. This model takes into account the influence of genetic factors, of friends and family, and of self-esteem in the development of the addiction. All three models—psychological, disease, and social learning—recognize the powerful psychological component of addiction. Most detailed definitions of addiction are a combination of these three theories. Addiction is discussed at length in Chapter 3.

Alcohol has always been popular with human beings, and apparently it always caused problems for some people. As far back as 32 B.C., the Greek philosopher Aristotle wrote essays on the abuse of drink. Today, 15 million adults are believed to experience problems from alcohol use alone. It is the drug of

The Extent of the Problem

In an average month in 1994:

- ❑ 13 million people used illicit drugs.

- ❑ 10 million used marijuana, making it the most commonly used illicit drug.

- ❑ 1.4 million used cocaine.

- ❑ 13 million had five or more drinks per occasion on five or more days in the month.

- ❑ 40 million people, including 4 million adolescents age twelve to seventeen, smoked cigarettes.[3]

choice among teenagers. In a 1992 national study, 70 percent of young people reported having tried alcohol by the eighth grade. One-half of all traffic fatalities involve alcohol, and it is a factor in over half of all violent deaths in this country.[4] Other drugs cause serious problems for our population, but none has the broad impact of ethyl alcohol.

Tobacco use has been recognized as one of the major public health hazards of the twentieth century. People have been smoking and chewing tobacco for hundreds of years, but the link between smoking and disease was not understood until the mid-1960s. Tobacco use declined as people began to understand the enormous risks associated with it. A massive antismoking campaign, fueled by the results of studies on the health hazards of secondhand smoke, has permanently changed the smoking behavior of Americans, and even the laws governing the use of tobacco. However, nicotine, the highly addictive drug in tobacco, still has a hold on millions of Americans. In fact, alcohol and tobacco cause more problems for our society than all other drugs combined.[5]

Many experts in the field of drug education consider alcohol and tobacco gateway drugs. They believe that young people learn about abusing substances by drinking and smoking and that these activities may stimulate interest in more powerful drugs like marijuana, cocaine, LSD, and heroin.[6] People who use these potent drugs are seeking more intense highs (mind-altering experiences) than they have been able to achieve with tobacco or alcohol. The addiction potential is also increased in these powerful drugs.

Addictions to drugs and alcohol have powerful effects on the addicts, their families, and their communities. These addictions are often associated with crimes, violence, and murders.

The impact substance abuse has on our society is demonstrated by the following statistics from a study done at Brandeis University:

- Each year, nearly half a million Americans die from alcohol, tobacco, and illicit drugs, making substance abuse the single largest preventable cause of death in the country.

- A person dying from alcohol-related causes loses, on average, twenty-six years off the normal life span; drug-related causes, over thirty-seven years; and smoking-related causes, about twenty years.

- At least half the people arrested for major crimes— including homicide, theft, and assault—were using illicit drugs at the time of their arrest.

☐ AIDS among injecting drug users is the fastest growing cause of death among substance abusers.

☐ One half to two thirds of homicides and serious assaults involve alcohol.

☐ Nearly 20 percent of men and 25 percent of women say that drinking has been a cause of trouble in their family.

☐ One out of every three divorced women was married at one time to a problem drinker.

☐ Alcohol alone cost the nation $99 billion in 1990. These costs are related to lost productivity as a result of illnesses, accidents, and deaths.[7]

Addictions of Behavior

An addiction of behavior is an activity that is out of control. The person involved in an addiction of behavior chooses doing it over anything else, no matter what effect the choice has on his or her life. For example, a person addicted to gambling might choose to gamble with money needed to buy food for the family. A person addicted to eating will ignore the dangers of obesity, physicians' warnings, or the concerns of family and friends. Addictions of behavior are less often seen as problems by our society than addictions to drugs and alcohol, in part because they are activities common to everyday life. Everyone eats, for example, and gambling is a popular recreation. The problems caused by behavioral addictions are often less visible and have less impact on society than addictions to drugs and alcohol, although they can be equally devastating to the addict and his or her family.

The people who most often feel the effects of an addict's behavior are family members. These are the people who must suffer the consequences of a gambler's losses. They are the people most likely to endure the abuse from an alcoholic or the neglect from someone consumed by gambling. Young children are especially vulnerable because they are not able to take care of themselves. Adolescents get trapped, feeling the need to take care of and support other family members.

Healthy Families

Families exist in our society as safe places to care for and nurture offspring. Healthy families offer all family members this safe place where there is unconditional love, physical and emotional support, and acceptance. These families know how to solve their conflicts, at least most of the time. They are forgiving of one another and support the uniqueness of family members. Children in these families are able to get their needs for food and warmth, love and affection, attention and fun met in appropriate ways. Flexibility is perhaps the most important characteristic of healthy families. They are able to change and adjust in the face of difficulties or to meet the changing needs of family members. Healthy families are like trees that are able to bend and flex in the storms of life and so are not uprooted.

Joanne's mother described this incident to Joanne's school counselor:

> We were eating dinner when Joanne dropped the bomb. She told us she wants to work a year before going to college. Her grandmother blew up. I was pretty upset too, because we've been saving for college since she was a baby. There was a lot of

yelling, but after a while we calmed down and talked about it. I never had the chance for a college education, and my mother and I really want this for Joanne. She insisted that she only wanted a year. She thinks it will give her time to decide what she wants to study. And . . . well, we decided to ask for this meeting, to find out what kinds of work she might be able to get.

This family was upset by the change in their teenager's college plans, and, in fact, became very angry with one another. They did, however, follow a healthy course of action. They were able to let go of the anger and discuss the issue. They were able to talk and to listen, and they were able to seek information that would help them reach a solution.

Families of Addicts

The family of an addicted adult is, at least some of the time, not a safe or nurturing place for children. The very survival of the family may be threatened by the behavior of the addicted person. The addict has no time to be involved with the family or to meet any responsibilities toward the family because he or she is so involved with the addiction. Most addictions cost money, and the addict will sacrifice anything, even the needs of the family, to take care of the addiction. The family system of an addict is out of balance, and the whole family becomes involved in trying to get the family back in balance.

In such situations, the focus is on keeping the family going, not on the needs of individual family members. These families are stuck trying to survive. Change is seen as a threat to the family's survival. This resistance to change has the greatest impact on adolescents, who are going through the most important physical, mental, and emotional changes of their lives.

Michael is another student who is preparing for college. He shared this story with a support group for families of drug addicts: "I want to study oceanography at a university near the coast. My dad won't even talk about it. He is all ready to sign me up for his old college . . . in accounting! He has said . . . if I do anything else, I can write him out of my life."

Michael's father is addicted to cocaine. His addiction has caused him to lose several good jobs and led to the breakup of his marriage to Michael's mother. His life is out of control, and he is attempting to control Michael in an effort to feel in charge again. The ironic thing about this behavior is that controlling Michael will not actually affect his father's life. It will, however, briefly give him the illusion of control. Michael's needs are not being considered here, but he is profoundly affected by his father's controlling behavior. This family is not talking. Family members are not being heard. In fact, Michael is truly afraid of losing his father if he tries to pursue oceanography.

There is a major difference in the way Joanne and Michael act toward their families. Joanne is not afraid to bring up a subject that she knows is likely to upset her family. She is confident, from her past experiences, that she will have an opportunity to express her views. Michael, on the other hand, has no such expectation. He is afraid of his father's reaction to his views on college.

Addicts' families have several characteristics that keep them from getting the help they often need. Addictions, which are very expensive, are a real drain on family finances. These families may be focused on

Changes in Family Health

Healthy families and addicts' families vary in the ways their members relate to each other. The following chart defines some common characteristics of both kinds of families:

Healthy Families	Addicts' Families
Flexible/open to change	Rigid, fixed rules
Respect differences in family members	Family members are assigned roles
Open communication; able to express feelings	Many secrets; strong feelings not permitted
Respect for individuals, privacy, and boundaries	Lack of privacy; little respect for personal feelings
Sense of humor	Little humor except to make fun of others
Argue and resolve conflicts	Pretend they don't have conflicts, forbid them, or ignore them
Strong sense of belonging	Feeling of isolation, aloneness

survival, concerned only with keeping a roof over their heads and food on the table.

The addict is often an embarrassment to the family, a source of shame. The family may strive to keep the addiction a secret. Family members may not even talk about it among themselves . . . acting as if the problem does not exist.

Having to keep this shameful secret means hiding the addicted person from other people as much as possible. Children from these families may avoid bringing friends home for fear of revealing the secret. In fact, the family may isolate itself from friends, community groups, and even more distant family members who could offer help and support.

There is no typical addict's family. Some families appear normal and are able to function fairly well for a long time, even when one person is addicted. In Melissa's family, the drinking went on for some time before her father lost his job and they were forced to move. Other families have problems that are so severe that they spill out into public view. The news is full of such problems. An accountant who is addicted to gambling embezzles money from his company. A teenager is arrested in a drug bust. Drunk drivers kill people every day, and their alcoholism becomes public knowledge.

Addicts do not start out with the intention of hurting their families or of destroying their own lives. They start out choosing to do activities or use substances that help them to feel good or not to feel bad. Once they are addicted, they are no longer choosing, but feel compelled to do the activity or use the substance, no matter what the effect on themselves or the people they love. The families of addicts react to

Melissa

(Melissa is a child of alcoholic parents. She continues her story for this book.)

I remember when I was very little, how much fun my parents seemed to have. They had parties on weekends at our house, or they went out and came home late at night being loud and silly. Sometimes, they would go out during the week, but in those days, that was unusual. We would have dinner together, all five of us, and then my brothers and I would do our homework, and Mom and Dad would watch T.V. Then, very gradually, our lives started to change. My parents started drinking at home every night. They called it the cocktail hour. My brothers and I began to have dinner alone in the kitchen, while my parents had their cocktails in the living room. They would talk, watch the news, and, sometimes, have a friend or two in to join them. I remember wondering if they ate dinner, because when I went to bed they were still drinking.

But we still had fun in those days. Birthdays and holidays were especially wonderful. The house would be full of people on Christmas and Thanksgiving. My mother would make little sandwiches and cakes to serve when people came by, and sometimes she would let me help her. For birthdays we went to fancy restaurants to celebrate. Then, when I was about eight, I realized that my parents had stopped being silly or talking when they were drinking and started fighting. They argued all the time. Sometimes they screamed at my brothers and me to get out and leave them alone. It really scared me, and I started hiding in my closet so they wouldn't yell at me. They fought about everything . . . who drank the most, who was spending too much money, who was at fault for all our troubles. I didn't know we had money problems until they started fighting. I guess they were spending a lot on alcohol and parties. They yelled at my middle brother, Tony, for asking for too much, or not being helpful enough, or causing them more problems. I tried hard not to bother them at all.

My oldest brother, Sean, took a paper route to help out with money. When I needed something, I usually asked him for the money to buy it. Tony was getting to be a real pain. He started getting into all kinds of trouble at school. By the time I was twelve, I was taking care of myself. My parents were drunk a lot of the time, so I didn't bring friends home, and I never had the money to go to the movies or out for pizza. I felt like I was always on the outside looking in.

The funny thing is that in spite of trash cans full of beer and gin bottles piled up by the back door, my family never mentioned the words drinking or drunk. In fact, we never even talked about all the fighting and screaming. It was a family rule. Another rule was not to tell anyone about the drinking or the fighting. I don't ever remember being told that; I just seemed to know not to mention it to anyone. When I was a teenager, I remember telling people at school that my mother was sick to explain why I couldn't go anywhere and why they couldn't come to my house.

I didn't get very good grades. I loved to read, but I was no good at math or science. No one in my family really said much about it. My father would look at my report card and sigh and shake his head. I remember thinking that if I could just do better in school, things would be better at home. I felt responsible, somehow, for my family's problems.

My father finally lost his job because of his drinking, and we had to sell the house and move into a tiny apartment. I slept on the couch and had my things in a corner of my brothers' room. There was no privacy and no place to hide. I stayed away as much as possible. It was the only way I knew to survive.

the behavior of addicts in ways that help hold the family together. Their actions are not wrong and, in fact, may work very well to keep families going; they are just not helpful to healthy growth and development.

The first eighteen years of a young person's life are shaped by what happens in his or her family. Young people only know what they live, and whatever their family experience is, they may grow up to repeat it. Teenagers can learn healthy ways of living, however, whatever their family background.

Resilient Teenagers

Recent studies have explored the reasons that some young people who have difficult childhoods are successful in school and in relationships, and others are not. Experts have identified characteristics that they refer to as "characteristics of resiliency."[8] The word resilience means the ability to adapt, to be flexible, and to bounce back. Young people with these characteristics overcome family problems, impoverished and dangerous neighborhoods, and poor schools to become successful.

Not only do most of the studies on resiliency identify the presence of these qualities, but studies of people with mental illness, addiction problems, and criminal records consistently identify the lack of these traits.

Researchers have discovered that children who are even-tempered and good-natured are more likely to survive a difficult or stressful childhood successfully. These children are well liked by others and so are able to get some of their needs for attention, love, and belonging met outside the family.

Resilient teenagers . . . think for themselves

. . . resist put-downs

. . . have a sense of humor

. . . are forgiving

. . . build satisfying friendships

. . . are optimistic

. . . are persistent

. . . avoid getting overly involved
   in other people's problems

. . . ask for help

However, there are many other factors that play a significant role in the development of resiliency. A close, caring, and supportive relationship with one adult (not necessarily a parent), for example, provides powerful protection for children living in deprived or dysfunctional homes. Children whose families and/or communities have high expectations for them grow up with a belief in themselves and a sense of hope that can override the most difficult living circumstances. One study looked at the child survivors of the Holocaust to determine why many of them were able to go on to lead full productive lives. This study concluded that a sense of hope and expectation for the future enabled these children to grow into productive adults.[9]

The opportunity for meaningful participation is another means of developing resiliency in young people. Children who are actively involved in the life and work of the family and/or community in responsible and productive ways are more likely to feel valued and capable. Numerous studies on resilient children may help to explain why only one in four children from an alcoholic home becomes an alcoholic. They may explain the hundreds of thousands of success stories of people who have risen out of childhoods of profound poverty, abuse, and neglect.[10]

Exploring Addiction's Impact

This book is an exploration of addiction and its impact on the families of addicts. It is important to the understanding of addiction and the profound effect it may have on family members first to develop a concept of family and to understand how members interact with one another. A family is a kind of system. It also has a structure, rules of conduct, and patterns of behavior and interaction that are uniquely its own. The family system, the way the family works and relates, is its identity, and the family will tend to resist any change in its identity.[11] The next chapter is a discussion of the family system.

Addiction has an impact on the family system in ways that require family members either to change as a family or adjust to the addiction. Chapter 3 looks at the process of addiction and why the impact of addiction on the family is often so profound. You will see in Chapter 4 that developing specific roles for members of addicts' families helps families to try to manage the addiction while at the same time avoiding change.

Addicted teenagers cause some unique problems for families; these are explored in Chapter 5. Because their parents or caregivers are still responsible for them, it is actually easier for teenage addicts to avoid taking responsibility for their behavior. Also, because the addiction interferes with the physical, emotional, and intellectual maturing that ordinarily takes place in adolescence, these young people may not be prepared to support themselves, and they may continue to be dependent on family members well into adulthood.

For these teenagers, and for all members of addicted families, there is hope and help. Chapter 6 is a discussion of the numerous resources in school and in the community available to young people and their families. For young people who see themselves in some of the stories told in this book, helping resources are listed in Chapter 6.

2

Families as Systems

☐ Do you live with your grandparents?

☐ Are you adopted?

☐ Are your cousins like brothers and sisters to you?

☐ Does your family have close friends who are considered part of the family?

How would you define the word *family*? Whom would you include? Traditionally, Americans have defined family as a mother and a father and one or more children. *Extended family* in this traditional definition includes grandparents, aunts, uncles, and cousins, all related by blood or marriage. Now, at the close of the twentieth century, this definition applies to only 25 percent of the families in this country. Half of all American households are headed by a single parent. Another 25 percent of families are a diverse mix of adults and children, related and unrelated.[1]

Defining the Family

The United States Census Bureau looks at households, the number of adults and children living under one roof, as family units. People who are unrelated live together as roommates or housemates in order to share expenses or for emotional support. Foster children live with adult caregivers who are not their biological parents. There are communes all over this country where people who are unrelated come together in support of a particular lifestyle or a particular set of beliefs and call themselves a family. Schools consider a student's family to be those people who are legally responsible for the student, unless the student has been declared independent by the courts. An independent minor is responsible for himself or herself.

Society is struggling to adapt to changes in living patterns. In some communities, homosexual and lesbian couples who are in long-term relationships and share a home are being afforded the same tax advantages as married couples. Single adults who meet certain requirements can now adopt children, something unheard of twenty years ago. One child, in a well-publicized court case, was actually able to choose a family other than his biological family with which to live. Words like *committed, supportive,* and *nurturing* are now used side by side with *blood relative* and *marriage* to describe the relationships that form families. Numerous books now available assure children that it is okay for families to be different.

This poem, taken from a book for elementary school children, does so with enthusiasm:

> *John has a family of two*
> *Himself and his dear old Aunt Sue*
> *Angela's family is Daddy and Mom*
> *A sister named Kim and a brother called Tom*
> *Miguel has a family he numbers at ten*
> *Because each of his parents got married again.*
> *He now has four parents and step sisters three*
> *One more half brother and a baby named Lee.*
> *Andy has a family of seven we're told*
> *With some very young people and some very old.*
> *There's an uncle and cousin, a grandma and mother*
> *A dear baby sister and much older brother.*
> *There are some families big and some families small*
> *Some families related and some not at all.*
> *But there's one special thing that all of them share:*
> *Families are made up of people who care.*[2]

The family unit, whatever form it takes, is intended to meet many of the needs of its members. According to John Bradshaw, a psychologist in the field of family work, the family also exists to meet society's need for support of its values and rules.[3] Each family has its own procedures for functioning, but those procedures are influenced by the family members' ethnic origins, religion, traditions, and community.[4] The family teaches children ways to interact with others appropriately and other skills necessary for getting along in the world. It teaches children ways to meet life's problems and to deal with situations similar to patterns of family life established by the culture and community. These are the traditional patterns of family life that ensure that each family member's need for food, warmth, safety, love, belonging, and accomplishment is met and that children learn how to function in the larger world. Today, politicians, religious representatives, and other society leaders claim that because American families no longer do the job of preparing their children to live in our society, they are the cause of the increase in violence, drug use, and other crimes against society. This comparison with family life of earlier times is unfair to families of the present day, because society has changed drastically during the last fifty years.

Understanding Systems

For the purposes of this book, *families* will be defined as those people who live together under one roof. These people are a system, acting and interacting with one another every day.

One example of a system is the school system. Its function is to provide an education to all the children in its district. The system has a structure made up of a school board and superintendent, school buildings, teachers, principals and students, buses, books, and numerous people who tend to the everyday operation of the system. All these parts are connected. Many

Every family system . . .

- ☐ has structure and function
- ☐ is made up of individual parts
- ☐ connects its individual parts in specific ways for a common purpose

other people, such as cafeteria workers, the school nurse, maintenance people, and secretaries, work to make sure that the system operates smoothly every day. When one part of the system cannot do its job, what happens to the structure and function of the system? The school system, in order to be fully functional, must get the flawed part of the system working again or must find a way to replace it.

The human body is a system. Each of its many parts has a particular function. The heart moves blood through the arteries and veins, the hands grasp, and the brain thinks. Each part is connected to the others by tissue, muscle, and nerves. For the human body to function as a system, all the parts of the body must work together toward this common purpose. If one part of the body does not work well, the system must adjust or stop functioning.

In a family system, the parts are the individual members of the family. They connect through their relationships with one another. It is the way they communicate, the rules they live by, and the beliefs and values they uphold that form the family system. Each family member has an equally important, but different, role in the family system. When one family member does not want or is not able to do his or her part, the rest of the family must adjust to the change to keep the family going.

The Addict's Family System

"Families are like mobiles," claims author Murray Dubin. "Move one part and everyone else in the family moves."[5]

Think about what happens when one part of a

carefully balanced mobile is removed. The mobile becomes unbalanced, and all the parts stop working. The mobile cannot work again unless the remaining parts do the work of the missing piece or the piece is replaced.

A similar thing happens in a family in which there is addiction. The addicted family member cannot do his or her part in the family, and in fact makes it difficult for all the other members to do their parts. The addiction causes a severe imbalance in the family. The family may even start falling apart. In order for it to work again, members must step in and take on roles that will help them to make up for the problems the addict is causing.

Leonard is the oldest child in a family of five. He is an excellent student and well liked by everyone who knows him. The counselor who worked with Leonard did so with the intention of helping him get a scholarship to college. Leonard politely refused the offer, explaining that he was needed at home and had already looked into attending the community college at night. He helped his mother take care of his younger brothers and sisters and contributed money from two part-time jobs to help with food and other bills. His father, Leonard explained, was away a great deal. The counselor learned later that Leonard's father was an addicted gambler who had been in and out of jail for passing bad checks and selling stolen property. In order to keep the family functioning, Leonard had stepped in and taken on his father's role.

The addict's family will protect the addict from the consequences of his or her addictive behavior, do his or her work when necessary, and hide the problem from everyone outside of the immediate family in order not to upset the family system.

Judy Garland, a singer and actress best known for her role as Dorothy in the *Wizard of Oz*, struggled with drug addiction throughout her life. As a child star she was given amphetamines by studio doctors to help her control her weight. This early introduction to drugs began her lifelong battle with addiction. Her two daughters, Liza Minnelli and Lorna Luft, were in the battle with her. Liza Minnelli's first husband explains: "As kids, Liza and Lorna had regular sessions emptying out Judy's sleeping capsules and refilling them with sugar." Judy Garland's children, like so many other relatives of addicts, tried to protect their mother from the consequences of her addiction. Their story vividly demonstrates how the families of addicts become involved in the addictions of their family members.[6]

Rigid Family Rules

The families of addicts also set up very rigid rules to keep things going. Change is not allowed. These families have systems so precariously balanced that they fear that any change, any shift in the system, will destroy the family.

In the first chapter, Melissa talked about the rules in her alcoholic parents' family: "My family never mentioned the words *drinking* or *drunk*. In fact, we never even talked about the fighting and screaming. It was a family rule. Another rule was not to tell anyone about the drinking or the fighting."

"Don't talk" is a common rule in these family systems. If they did not talk about the addiction in

Melissa's family, it was much easier to ignore. If they talked about the drinking, and about the fighting and screaming associated with it, they would face and ultimately deal with the problems the behavior was causing.

"Don't feel" is another rule in Melissa's family that she did not mention in her story. If the family had talked about the fighting and screaming, they also would have had to talk about feelings of anger and fear that caused it. It is typical that these families avoid talking about feelings, because so many of those feelings are painful.

A third rule of the family systems of addicts is "Don't trust." Addictive behavior is unpredictable and selfish. Children in these families learn not to believe what adults tell them and not to expect or anticipate.

Tonya joined a suicide support group at her school and shared her family's story:

> I have never counted on anyone but myself. My dad is busy all the time, and my mother lives in another state. Even when I had to go to the hospital for appendicitis, the school nurse took me there and signed me in, and a neighbor picked me up when I was allowed to go home. Dad called, but he never came to see me. We mostly talk on the phone, even though we live in the same house. He is always promising great trips and new clothes, but he almost never even remembers my birthday. I really don't believe anything he says anymore. I guess that's why I thought about suicide. It's as if I am all alone, and nobody cares what happens to me.

Tonya's dad is not there for her. He is compulsively involved in activities that seem to be more important to him than keeping his promises to his daughter. His treatment of Tonya is unpredictable and selfish. It is easier for Tonya to expect nothing from him than constantly to be disappointed.

Family Rules

There are three rules that help keep the family systems of addicts together.

- ☐ Don't talk
- ☐ Don't trust
- ☐ Don't feel

As long as the family follows these rules, it will not have to deal with the problems the addiction is causing.

Change and the Family System

Everyday events can cause changes in the family:

- ☐ Dad gets a new job that takes him out of town during the week.

- ☐ Aunt Susan dies.

- ☐ There is a divorce or a new baby.

- ☐ Someone in the family goes away to school or gets married.

In each of these situations, the family system has to adjust to the change. Even situations that are temporary change the family system. When Grandma comes for a visit, a family member may have to give up his or her bedroom and move in with a younger brother or sister. It may mean more arguments between the children in

Nothing Stays the Same

What changes have you experienced in your family? Has a family member moved in or out of your house? Has someone had a new baby, married, or died? List these events on a piece of paper. Using the changes on your list as a guide, write how each event affected your family system.

☐ Did any of the events change the way members of your family go about their lives?

☐ How did the change directly affect you?

☐ Were the changes permanent?

the family, because they are not used to sleeping together. A new baby brings a permanent change to the family system. Each of the other children may have to take on more responsibilities, the family may have less money to spend, and everyone will have less of mother's time.

Understanding your family system is a way of understanding yourself. It helps to explain the differences as well as the similarities between family members. Your family, the way its members relate to one another, their values, and their beliefs, all have a great deal to do with who you are and what you will become.

3

The Disease of Addiction

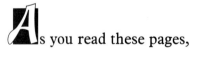s you read these pages,

- a student in your school is chewing breath mints to hide the smell of alcohol. She has it all figured out, how she can hide vodka in a bottle labeled as spring water. She puts the bottle on her desk, right under the teacher's nose, and sips from it all day long. She gets a buzz, the euphoric feeling of detachment that she craves constantly. While she is in school, her parents are worrying about their daughter's drop in grades and her strange mood swings. They know something is terribly wrong, but they are not sure what it is.

- a neighbor is pawning his family's stereo in order to pay a gambling debt. He told the family he was taking the stereo to be repaired. With the money he gets from the pawnshop, he will only be able to pay one of his debts, and before the day is out he will owe still more money. He cannot stop himself and is rapidly putting his family in serious financial trouble. His wife and son are filled with dread each time the phone rings, for fear that yet another creditor is calling.

someone in your community is bingeing. Her children are in school, and the house is dark and quiet. The light of the refrigerator comes on as she opens the door to get something to eat. Again and again the refrigerator light flashes on as she continues to eat until the food is gone. She cannot stop eating, even though her health is in jeopardy. She craves food more than anything else in her life. Her children are neglected, unclean, and malnourished.

Someone who is addicted has an intense relationship with an activity or a substance. If you have ever fallen in love, you may understand some of the feelings the addict experiences. When you first fall in love with someone, you want to be with that person constantly. Time away from your love interest is spent thinking about him or her and planning ways to be with the person again. In fact, nothing in life is as interesting or as exciting as being with the one you love in the early stages of your relationship. The addict behaves similarly, spending a great deal of time, money, and energy being involved with the addiction. The addiction becomes the focus of the addict's life, more important or valuable than any person, event, or undertaking. In most love relationships, feelings eventually stabilize and become less intense. The addict's obsession with the substance or activity, however, remains the focus of his or her life until disaster, death, or help intervenes.

People become addicted to particular activities by trying to control their feelings. They may discover, for example, that betting on races helps them to forget their worries. They may learn that having a drink with friends makes them feel good. In either case, these people repeat the experience when they need to forget or want to feel good. When these people overdo—miss a family celebration because they were at the track, drink too much and pass out, or go on a spending or eating binge—they have feelings of guilt about the behavior. They may feel embarrassed or ashamed or even depressed because they were out of control.

The behavior that embarrasses or depresses them is the same behavior that helps them to forget and to feel good. Addicts get into a cycle of using the substance or doing the activity to forget or feel better, only to feel ashamed or depressed afterward. Once into this cycle, they begin to deny that it is their out-of-control behavior that is making them feel bad or causing problems in their lives. They blame others or circumstances for what is happening to them.

Characteristics of Addiction

People who become addicted repeat the experience or use the substance over and over again. They develop a tolerance to the activities they are involved in, meaning that they have to increase their involvement to achieve the same feelings they got when they first started the activity.

As addicts become more involved in their addictions, their behavior is likely to attract the attention of family members or friends. Addicts often develop elaborate schemes to hide the extent of their addiction from others. As they begin deceiving their family and friends, they also deceive themselves. As involvement in the addiction accelerates, so do the problems caused by the addiction. To avoid facing these problems, and thus having to deal with the addiction that caused them, addicts build a wall of denial that separates them from the consequences of their behavior. Breaking down the wall of denial is the first step an addict must take to begin treatment.

The Power of Addiction

A good example of the power of addiction is in the description of the wedding of Jacqueline Bouvier to John F. Kennedy, our thirty-fifth president, in the best-selling book *The Kennedy Women: The Saga of an American Family*. Jackie's father, Blackjack Bouvier, did not appear at her wedding to walk her down the aisle as planned. He was back at the hotel, too intoxicated to attend. Jacqueline Kennedy's father was addicted to alcohol, and even for an event as important as his daughter's wedding, he could not overcome his need to drink.[1]

The movie *Fatal Attraction* is an excellent example of the power a relationship addiction has over the addict. One character becomes obsessed with another, to the extent that all other aspects of her life become unimportant. Her need for the relationship takes over her life, and when he tries to break up with her she attempts to kill him. Her addiction overwhelms her conscience and whatever moral code or beliefs she valued.

All the activities listed above, except using illegal drugs, are considered normal in our society. Moderate

Common Addictions

☐ Drinking alcohol

☐ Using drugs

☐ Gambling

☐ Spending money

☐ Sex/relationships

☐ Eating

consumption of alcohol is permissible, and even gambling is considered acceptable recreation. The activities themselves do not cause problems. However, when people are involved in these activities to meet needs that should be met through healthy relationships with others, or are involved to the extent that they neglect other aspects of their lives, they are showing signs of addiction, and they create difficulties for themselves and their families.

Causes of Addiction

Most people can have experiences with alcohol and other drugs, with gambling or eating, and not become addicted. Exactly what causes one person to eat or spend compulsively and another person to eat or spend normally is not entirely understood. Most

How Addiction Happens

Addictions follow a predictable course. The stages are:

Casual activity, experimental use. In this phase, a person is introduced to the substance or the activity. For example, most people try alcohol and tobacco for the first time in their teen years.[2] Each time the person tries the activity or substance, he or she learns something more about it. People who try alcohol may learn that it makes them feel relaxed or gives them headaches. Someone who gambles may find it very exciting or anxiety causing. What these people learn from casual experimental activities determines whether they will continue to be involved. There are many people who tried cigarettes at some time in their lives and do not smoke, or who tasted alcohol and do not drink. Those that continue like the feelings the activity produces and seek to have those feelings again.

According to Robert DuPont, people between the ages of twelve and twenty are vulnerable to all the outside forces that will influence their decisions about alcohol and other drugs.[3]

Regular, routine activity or use. In this phase, the person begins to incorporate the activity into his or her life. Someone who gambles may wager a certain amount every week on races or sporting events. Time for eating that is in addition to mealtimes, becomes part of the overeater's day. Earlier, Melissa recalled that cocktail hour became a routine activity for her parents. The activity has increased in importance in the person's life. Tolerance may begin to develop in people using drugs and alcohol, meaning that they must increase the use of the substance to get the desired effect. However, the person doing the activity or using the drug is still in control during this time. At this point, he or she can choose to stop. Some people stay at this stage of involvement, never moving on to dependency.

Dependency. It is during this phase that the person involved in the activity begins to lose control. The activity has reached such a high level of importance in the person's life that he or she begins to believe that involvement is necessary. People who are dependent plan their lives to ensure that they are able to do the activity or use the substance. For people dependent on illegal drugs, this phase is particularly involved. These people must find sources for their drugs, ensure that there is money regularly available to purchase them, and manage to obtain the drugs regularly without getting caught. People addicted to prescription drugs have similar involvement. They may regularly have to change physicians and drugstores in order to continue having the drugs prescribed. This involvement takes time and money.

Addiction. Everything in the person's life is now directed toward using the substance or doing the activity. The person is no longer in control and things that were once important in life are sacrificed to the addiction. The urge to be involved with the addictive substance or activity overwhelms addicts. It is more powerful than their consciences, their value systems, or even their physical need for rest or food. Once honest, honorable people will break the law to support the addiction, stealing money to buy drugs or to pay a gambling debt.[4]

research on addiction is about addiction to alcohol and other drugs.

Experts who have studied substance abuse have learned that age of first use has a great deal to do with whether or not a person becomes addicted. Teenagers who reported experimenting with drinking or drugs prior to the age of fifteen were "more likely" to become abusers as those who experimented after the age of fifteen.[5]

Addiction also moves from generation to generation in families. A grandmother may be addicted to food, her son may be addicted to alcohol, and her grandson may be a compulsive gambler. The addictions are different, but the behaviors are the same. All these people are using an activity to feel good and to stop feeling bad. Chances are that the son promised himself that he would never be fat, but he learned from his mother's example that compulsive activity is the way to deal with feelings. Alcohol helped him forget his worries and feel good about himself. The grandson probably promised himself that he would not miss out on life by drinking all the time, but he too had learned about compulsive behavior from his father and his grandmother. He discovered gambling as a way of handling his feelings.

Gambling and eating are psychological addictions, because the addicts believe they must be involved in those particular activities to feel good or not to feel bad. People addicted to alcohol and other drugs are physically addicted as well as psychologically addicted. Over time, the body of the user develops a need for the alcohol or other drugs. These substances are constantly present in the body of a person who uses daily, and the body eventually adjusts to the presence of the new chemical. Once it has made the adjustment, it cannot function properly without the drug. You may have seen addicts on television or in the movies who are sweating, writhing in pain, and very sick. They are going through withdrawal because their bodies are not getting the drugs they need to function properly. In fact, most drug addicts will tell you that they no longer take drugs to feel good, but rather to avoid withdrawal. They continue to use drugs to avoid feeling bad.

People at Risk

Children of drug addicts and alcoholics are at great risk for becoming addicted themselves. Research tells us that in addition to learning to use drugs and alcohol at home, these children may have inherited a gene for addiction. Experts have now identified a gene that male children of alcoholic fathers inherit that can cause alcoholism.[6] (It is important to note here that for alcoholism to occur, an individual must first choose to drink.) They believe that there is also a gene that can cause alcoholism in female children of alcoholics, but it has not yet been studied. This information is simply telling us that children of alcoholics and drug addicts are at much greater risk for becoming addicted themselves than children of people who are not addicted. People who have a history of heart disease in their family are at high risk of a heart attack or stroke. Knowing this information allows people to take steps, such as watching their diets or exercising, to reduce the risk. The same can be said of people who have a history of addiction in their family. They too can take steps, such as avoiding addictive drugs, to reduce or eliminate the risk.

Substance-Exposed Children

Some children have no control over whether or not they are exposed to addictive drugs. These children are exposed to alcohol or other drugs in utero (before birth) and are born addicted to and/or developmentally damaged by the substances their mothers used.

The drugs taken by these women affect the developing fetuses in ways that can be permanent or temporary, obvious or subtle.[7] Children exposed to frequent or heavy alcohol use before birth, for example, may be born with a group of characteristics known as fetal alcohol syndrome (FAS). These babies have growth deficiencies, mental retardation, and malformed facial features. Babies of cocaine-addicted mothers may be born addicted themselves and suffer withdrawal symptoms immediately after birth. Low birth weight, irritability, poor feeding, and sleeplessness are other problems suffered by many of these newborns. Studies have consistently indicated that children born to smokers have lower birth weights and are more likely than children of nonsmokers to have learning and behavior problems in their early years.[8]

Experts are not clear about what amount of a drug will cause problems for the unborn child or when during development the fetus will be affected by a particular drug, but they do know that a woman who uses drugs while she is pregnant is taking an enormous risk.[9] Expectant women are now instructed by their physicians to avoid alcohol, cigarettes, and most kinds of prescription and nonprescription drug.

Substance-exposed children of addicts have two strikes against them. They are born developmentally affected by alcohol or other drugs and into the family chaos of an addict.

Signs of Possible Addiction

Certain behaviors, like those listed here, may indicate an addiction:

1. The person would rather drink, eat, gamble, and so on, than spend time with a family member or a friend.
2. The person keeps increasing the amount of time that is spent drinking, eating, gambling, and so on.
3. The person forgets or ignores family events such as birthdays and visits from friends because of his or her involvement with the activity.
4. The person seems to be unable to control the amount of time spent doing the activity.
5. The person, when unable to do the activity, becomes irritable, moody, tearful, angry, or hostile.
6. The person hides the activity or the substance from family and friends.
7. The person denies having a problem, when many things obviously are going wrong.
8. The person has extreme moods swings that are completely unpredictable.
9. The person blames other people for his/her troubles and does not take responsibility for his/her own actions.
10. The person uses alcohol or other drugs and blacks out (forgets large chunks of time).
11. The person has headaches, stomach disorders, and other unexplained and ongoing physical symptoms.
12. The person begins to neglect his/her appearance and to do hurtful or illegal things.[10]

None of these things alone indicates that someone is addicted. The statements are simply descriptions of the kinds of behaviors and attitudes that are typical of an addicted person. Most people are not alcoholics, drug addicts, sex or relationship addicted, or addicted to gambling. Most people participate in one or more of these activities regularly or occasionally without becoming addicted.

Remember learning about Melissa's family in the first chapter? Melissa recalled that her parents seemed to be having fun partying when she was a little girl. This was the stage when her parents were drinking to feel good and to avoid feeling bad. The more they drank, the more their addiction affected the family. Melissa remembers when her parents began to fight about money. She recalls her own fear of their anger and her need to hide from it. In Melissa's family, the income, the family relationships, and the individuals in the family were all affected by the parents' addiction.

Michael's Story

Michael was introduced in the first chapter. His father, Harold, is addicted to cocaine. As Michael shared his story with his support group, the pattern of his father's addiction emerged:

Michael's father, Harold, was a successful attorney. He and Michael's mother were very active in the social circles of the community. Their friends were all equally successful professionals. The recreational use of cocaine was an accepted activity in these circles. Most house parties offered the use of alcohol, cocaine, and marijuana as part of the evening's entertainment.

Harold came to look forward to these events, and he and Michael's mother even hosted some of these parties themselves. It was not difficult at that time to get cocaine if one had the money, and Harold did.

The parties were being held more and more often; then Michael's mother decided she no longer wanted to be involved. Harold began attending alone, often staying away for the entire weekend. He would return home on Sunday night exhausted and belligerent, blaming Michael's mother for the way he was feeling. Michael tells of hearing his parents fight about the parties and about Harold's increasing use of the drug, and of hearing his father insist that cocaine helped him deal with the pressures of his job. Michael's mother expressed her fear of the effect the cocaine was having on Harold's personality and on their family life.

Michael said that it seemed as if his father's cocaine use increased every day. There were times when Harold skipped work to search neighboring towns for someone to sell him the drugs. Harold insisted that cocaine gave him a boost, and that the drug was not a problem for him.

Experts have studied the effects of cocaine on humans and can explain Harold's "boost" when using it. Cocaine is absorbed into the bloodstream very quickly and usually within ten minutes it has reached the pleasure center of the brain. The drug stimulates the brain in ways that produce feelings of euphoria and energy (the high) in the user. The feelings last anywhere from ten to thirty minutes depending on the user's tolerance for cocaine, whether the drug is injected, snorted, or smoked, and how strong it is.[11]

Harold needed more and more cocaine to maintain

his high. The fights between Michael's parents were escalating, and Michael's mother threatened to leave if Harold did not stop using cocaine. Finally, one day, Michael's mother did leave. Michael stayed with his father in order to finish high school. Shortly after that, Harold's law firm asked for his resignation, citing his neglect of responsibilities to his clients.

Michael's father still has a law license and continues to work as a legal consultant. Most of his time, however, and all of his money is spent finding, buying, and using cocaine. Michael spends weekdays at his father's house and weekends with his mother in a neighboring town. His mother gives him the money he and his father need to live on each week.

Harold has been in treatment for cocaine addiction, and Michael has attended some of his therapy sessions with him. Unfortunately, Harold has been unable to stay away from cocaine for more than a few weeks at a time.

Social Acceptance of Addiction

As addiction becomes better understood, it becomes less tolerated by our society. For example, drunkenness, which was considered entertaining enough to be included in humerous television shows and movies as late as the 1970s, is no longer seen as amusing behavior. Society has recognized the seriousness and the dangers of intoxication. Legal restraints on drinking have increased, as have the consequences in many states for driving under the influence of alcohol or for serving alcohol to minors.

Smoking, a popular activity in previous decades, is no longer permissible in most public places. A society that once considered smoking a sign of sophistication now for the most part views it as foolish, self-destructive behavior.

Percent of the U.S. Population That Smokes

1965 . . . . 42%
1974 . . . . 37%
1980 . . . . 33%
1985 . . . . 30%
1990 . . . . 26%
1991 . . . . 26%

Source: National Health Interview Surveys 1974–1991. Data compiled by the CDC Office on Smoking and Health: 1965 data from page 24.[12]

On the other hand, gambling is sanctioned by many states. In lotteries, casinos, on riverboats, and at racetracks, people are encouraged to bet money on the chance they will win more than the amount they wager. Most Americans participate in these activities at one time or another without being affected in any way. For those people who become addicted to gambling, however, the consequences are devastating.

Art Schlichter, former Ohio State quarterback and first-round National Football League draft pick in 1982, writes from a prison cell of his experiences as a gambling addict, remembering the first time he won big money, about three or four hundred dollars. In the article he tells how much he enjoyed the experience. Soon he was gambling every few days.

Art tells of his sophomore year in college and the pressure of being a football star. He remembers the gambling increasing as the pressure to perform increased. By then he was gambling every night, betting large sums of money taken from his savings. Gambling was becoming more important than anything in his life. He was neglecting his relationships, his school work, and even football, and was beginning to experience some of the problems that were resulting from this neglect.

This account of gambling addiction was written by Art Schlichter when he was a thirty-five-year-old man in prison for offenses committed to support his addiction. It demonstrates how long the addict's behavior may be tolerated by others. Art was, of course, famous for a short time, and famous people in our society are often permitted excesses that would ordinarily be frowned upon. Also, he was a gambler, and his betting behavior was not seen as abnormal for someone earning a National Football League salary.[13]

The Media's Influence on Behavior

Another acceptable behavior among Americans is self-medication with nonprescription and prescription drugs. Advertising and media encourage the quick fix for physical and psychological pain. As a result, our society has a low tolerance for discomfort and a tendency to look to drugs to treat every kind of problem.

Our culture sends mixed messages about sex and relationships. Soap operas and movies depict intense relationships and partners that change frequently.

Some of the most popular magazines and television shows have sex as their primary theme. In some cases, the media exploits and sensationalizes relationships and sexual addictions. The people who buy these magazines and tune in to these television programs in such large numbers are supporting this view of sexuality. Society, however, which is made up in part of these same people, conveys negative messages about divorce, makes adultery a crime in some states, and spends millions of dollars discouraging early and unprotected sex.

Our culture is changing, and with it the norms for behavior are changing. Gradually, we are beginning to understand the impact that addictive, compulsive behaviors have on our society.

4

Roles in Addicts' Families

Experts working in the field of addiction have identified roles that children in the families of addicts assume to help to balance the family system. Children take on these roles to survive in families that are not nurturing or protective. For example, a child may become a miniature adult, taking on many of the responsibilities of the addicted person in order to help maintain the family. A child may become reclusive or withdrawn from the family, sensing that the family cannot cope with another person with needs and feelings. These roles also serve as defense mechanisms for children, allowing them to ignore or deny their feelings of loneliness, anger, sadness, or resentment toward their addicted family members. Denial helps them to endure in abnormal, difficult, unhealthy, and sometimes even dangerous environments.

Finally, by taking on these roles to meet the needs of their addicted families, children meet some of their own needs for attention and belonging. Children in these families do not choose these roles consciously. They learn what behaviors gain acceptance for them in their families, and then they use those behaviors. People working in the field have labeled these roles in ways that help to describe the behaviors associated with them.[1]

The Scapegoat Child

Kim arrived at the counselor's office door seeking birth control information. She was dressed in a short leather skirt and boots that came up to her knees. Her black hair was streaked with orange and spiked into points on top of her head. Heavy makeup made her look much older than her fifteen years.

The counselor knew about Kim from meetings with the school Student Assistance Team. Kim had been referred during her freshman year for unexcused absences and during the first six-week period of the current year for failing three of her subjects. Attempts to bring Kim's mother into school to discuss these problems had not been successful.

"My mother is too spaced out to discuss anything," Kim said, when the counselor asked if she had talked to her mother about birth control. "She says she has bad nerves because of me." Kim went on to tell the counselor that her mother was addicted to tranquilizers and had been taking them regularly for several years, "ever since my brother graduated from high school. See, my parents separated about that same time. Mom was a zombie. They are back together again, and now they call me 'our problem child.' Can you just see me asking my mom about birth control? She already thinks I'm a lost cause."

The counselor remembered Kim's brother. He was a very bright, quiet, and unusually mature young man who had won an academic scholarship to a state university. In appearance, he was the complete opposite of the girl sitting in her office.

As Kim continued to talk, the counselor began to get a picture of the family. Kim's mother had been injured in a car accident when Kim was very small and received narcotic painkillers as part of her treatment. Kim remembers her mother taking painkillers for years after that, for the pain she said still existed from that accident. "The pills made her act dopey, like she couldn't understand what you were saying to her. And she would just sit there staring out a window or at the television. My father would come home and start yelling at me to get some food on the table. Somehow, it was always my fault that the house was a mess and we didn't have any food."

Eventually, Kim's mother ran out of doctors who were willing to prescribe the painkillers. "I was in the sixth grade that year, and my mother was having a really hard time without her pills. She yelled at me if I breathed wrong, and she was constantly telling my father how much trouble I was."

In the families of addicts, other family members often take on roles that help them and their families survive. Kim has the role of the scapegoat in her family: the family needs someone to blame for its problems, and Kim is meeting that need. With Kim in the family, they don't have to deal with the addiction of the mother or the conflict between the parents. They can blame Kim for the family's troubles.

"Finally, after about four months of feeling sick all the time, Mom went to see a psychiatrist. That's when she started on tranquilizers." That was also the year Kim's brother graduated and went off to college. He had been some support for her and a source of warmth and affection. When he left, Kim began to look outside the family to meet her needs for belonging and love. She has linked up with a group of high school dropouts, most of them drug users and all of them sexually active. In her survival role as the scapegoat, Kim has helped herself in a couple of ways. First, she is getting attention, although it is negative attention, with her outrageous dress and behavior. Second, she has found a way to get some of her needs for belonging and affection met while playing out this role.

Taking the Blame. Scapegoat children are very helpful in a family in which there is addiction. They take the blame for the family's problems, as Kim has done, and give the family something to focus on besides the addict and the addict's problems. They are especially important when the addict in the family is a parent. An addicted adult is an embarrassment, and the family will try to hide the problem for as long as possible. An acting-out child gives family members someone to point to and blame for any problems they are having. Kim's problems are also helping the family to stay together. Each time she does something outrageous, her parents are united in their bewilderment and anger.

Children who are scapegoats in addicts' families are the most likely of all children in these families to get into serious trouble with the legal system. As teenagers, they are inclined to drop out of school, have a low sense of responsibility for themselves or others, and are likely to be involved in addiction themselves. Often these teenagers started to act out at a very young age. Their reputation for difficult behavior follows them as they move through school.

Eventually it is not just the family that points to the young person as the problem, but also the school and the community. Their hostile, defiant behavior hides hurt and angry feelings. The scapegoat child feels responsible for the family's problems, and the family, by blaming the scapegoat, encourages that belief. People who heard what the cousins, aunts, uncles, and friends had to say about the family with a scapegoat child would very likely shake their heads in wonder that such a nice family could have had such a terrible child.[2]

Not all young people in trouble come from the families of addicts, but it is not unusual to find a difficult home life in the background of delinquents and dropouts. Scapegoat children are at great risk for abusing alcohol and other drugs at an early age, and teenage girls are at risk for becoming pregnant.

Getting Help. When the addict and the rest of the family are helped with the addiction problem, the scapegoat child is helped as well. When they get the help they need to deal with their painful feelings and lack of a sense of responsibility, scapegoat children grow up to be strong and generous people. They often become unusually courageous adults, able to deal easily with the highs and lows of life. Scapegoat children who are able to succeed make wonderful role models for children who are struggling. As adults, they are often found working either professionally or as volunteers with young people who are at risk for delinquency.[3]

The Hero Child

Remember Leonard, who appeared in Chapter 2? He is the hero in his family. Much like Kim's older brother, Leonard has taken on responsibilities that should belong to an adult. In some ways, Leonard has taken the place of his gambling addicted father in the family. He helps with the finances by working two jobs and, along with his mother, tries to parent his younger brothers and sisters. He was probably doing those things well before he became a teenager.

Hero children are very often the oldest children in the family. They are very responsible, often acting much older than their age. It is important for the addict's family to have something or someone to be proud of, and the hero child meets that need. Leonard does well in school and is liked by everyone. How can there be anything wrong with us, the family asks, if we have this wonderful child?

Someone to Hide Behind. Just as the addict's family hides behind the problems of the scapegoat child, it hides behind the hero child as well. The hero child gives the family value and worth. In spite of much more acceptable behavior, hero children have almost as many problems as scapegoats. By the time they become teenagers, their schools and communities are expecting the same responsible hard-working behaviors their families have come to depend on. In healthy families this behavior is not a problem, because the young people are successful in ways that meet their own needs. The hero's behavior meets the needs of the addict's family and, in fact, meets the needs of his or her teachers, coaches, and any others who come in contact with him or her, but does not necessarily meet the needs of the hero child.[4]

Burden of Unrealistic Expectations. Leonard is not being who he really is, but who the family needs him to be. The hero believes that somehow he or she should be able to fix the family's problems. Most hero children never feel good enough, no matter how smart, responsible, helpful, or successful they are. Some of those feelings may come from having to take on adult responsibilities at too young an age, or trying to meet unrealistic family expectations. The feeling of being inadequate may also come from the hero child's inability to "fix" the addicted parent.

Hero children are at very high risk of being addicted themselves, because they take on the roles of the addicted adults in their lives while they are still children.[5] They may marry addicts, because addictive behavior is so familiar to them and they are so accustomed to taking care of an addicted person. At the very least, they tend to be overly responsible and overly committed to other things and other people. Hero children make great executives and leaders, but often have to learn in adulthood how to relax and have fun.

The Lost Child

Melissa, who was introduced in the first chapter, is the child of two alcoholic parents. She learned at a very early age to stay out of the way when her parents were drinking. She is one member that her family does not have to worry about. Melissa is the lost child. She gets none of the attention in the family and does nothing to get attention. It is her role to make no demands on her family, but simply to stay out of the way. She has learned to be quiet, to keep her distance, and to avoid "rocking the boat" in her family. She is an expert at avoiding, hiding out, and disappearing. These are all survival skills for Melissa.

Playing Make-Believe. The trouble with these behaviors is that outside of the family, they cause some very real problems for Melissa. When she was younger, she would make up things about herself to tell to her classmates. She spent a great deal of time then playing make-believe, almost to the point of believing herself what she had made up. The other children made fun of her stories or called her a liar, which simply caused her to withdraw into her own world even more. As Melissa got older, she began living through the books she read.

Fading Into the Woodwork. Even now, at the age of eighteen, she is so quiet in school that the teachers sometimes forget she is there. She has difficulty making friends, spending most of her lunch hour reading in the library. As much as drama interests her, she would not dream of trying out for a play. Attempts by teachers to involve Melissa in classroom discussions have left her trembling in fear of having to speak up in front of others.

Melissa is not valued by her family and experiences feelings of worthlessness as a result. Melissa, like hero and scapegoat children, believes that she has some responsibility for the problems in her family. She explained:

> Somehow, I believed I had come out all wrong and had made my parents so unhappy that they had to drink and fight. I paid close attention to what they approved of or liked in other people and tried to be

those things. Those efforts, of course, didn't work to gain my parents' attention. When my brother was named to all-state in basketball, for example, my parents framed the newspaper clipping about him. The following year, I received an award from the literary society for a poem I had submitted. My picture was in the paper with a long article, which my parents did not even save, much less frame.

Without help, the lost child is at high risk for mental illness, especially depression. As teenagers, lost children are at especially high risk for suicide, in part because they are so often depressed. Lost children do not know how to ask for what they need, because their needs have always been ignored. They have no expectations for being noticed or appreciated. Any positive attention a lost child receives may be interpreted as love, whether it is appropriate attention or not. As they mature, these people get involved too easily, or never get involved in close relationships. They just don't know how to identify a healthy relationship.

However, this detachment from the family has a positive side. Lost children have lived by and within themselves for much of their lives, with limited interaction with other people. As a result, they are often imaginative and creative. When they are able to overcome feelings of worthlessness, they become very independent people who can develop and profit from their talents.[6]

The Mascot Child

Another role in addicts' families is that of the mascot. Frequently the youngest child, this individual provides comic relief, breaking the strain and tension that is so often present in the homes of these families. The family, in essence, uses the mascot to get some relief from the painful experiences of living with an addict.

Make 'em Laugh ... Class clowns are sometimes the mascots in their families. They have learned to meet their own need for attention and to meet the family's need to laugh by making jokes and clowning around. Just like other relatives of addicts, mascots carry the behavior with them to school. They are often willing to do almost anything for attention. Unlike the scapegoat, however, they rarely engage in behavior that gets them into serious trouble. Mascot children are cute and amusing, and teachers and family members, with small smiles on their faces, shake their heads and wonder what in the world to do about them.

Mascots meet their families' need for fun, but at the expense of their own needs to be who they are and to be taken seriously. They are afraid, like the rest of the family, that if they step out of their roles, their families will collapse. Like other children in these families, they feel some responsibility for family problems.[7]

As early as elementary school, mascot children may be misidentified as hyperactive, learning disabled, and immature. As mascots get older, they are at risk for developing ulcers and have difficulty handling stress.[8] They remain immature into adulthood, depending on the old childlike clowning to get along in the adult world. With help, mascots do mature, developing a sense of humor and a positive outlook on life that makes them delightful friends, coworkers, and spouses.

The Chief Enabler

Children in the families of addicts take on the roles discussed above to help themselves and their families survive. The role taken most often by the nonaddicted adult in the family is that of chief enabler. It is the role usually seen in the spouse or partner of the addicted person. When there is only one parent, an older child may take on the enabler role. This is the person who makes it possible for the addict to stay addicted. The enabler protects the addict from the consequences of his or her behavior.

The Enabler's Role

❑ The enabler makes excuses for the absence of the addicted person. (He is sick and can't go to work.)

❑ The enabler makes excuses for the addicted person's behavior. (She is very stressed and needs the medication.)

❑ The enabler takes on the addicted person's responsibilities or pulls in the hero child to help with those responsibilities. (I don't know what I would do without Leonard.)

❑ The enabler feels powerless. (What can I do about it?)

❑ The enabler often acts like a martyr. (I'll do it. I have to do everything around here anyway.)

The person who enables the addictive behavior of a spouse, parent, or child is not doing so intentionally to encourage the addiction, but rather to help the family survive. The enabler fears that if he or she does not cover up for the addicted person, the family will fall apart. The enabler takes on the responsibility for keeping the family going.[9]

However, it is the enabler who must get out of the way in order for the addict to get the help he or she needs. Until the enabler stops protecting the addict, the addict will not experience the consequences of addiction. Until an addict begins to experience those consequences, he or she cannot be helped. However, the consequences may be so horrible in the mind of the enabler that he or she cannot allow them to occur.

What often happens in families in which the addiction is being enabled by a well-meaning family member is that the enabling continues until something happens that cannot be ignored.

Inflexible Roles

The family system is fixed and rigid in addicts' families. The roles in these families are inflexible, which means that there is little or no opportunity for family members to grow or change. In Melissa's family, for example, she has the role of lost child. She is quiet and unobtrusive. Any effort on her part to change, perhaps to become more outgoing, would be discouraged or made fun of by her family. She would be pressured to stay in her role of lost child, because it is more important to maintain the family as it is than to meet the needs of individual family members.

People have roles in healthy families too. One

child might be thought of as the studious one in the family. Another child may be considered the athletic one. However, in healthy families, members are allowed and even encouraged to move in or out of roles as their needs and goals change. In a healthy family, Melissa, if she had a tendency to be quiet and distant, might be encouraged to be involved in activities that would help her to develop her social skills.

"Don't rock the boat" means just that in addicts' families. Family members hold the belief that the family will survive only if it stays the way it is. In order to maintain the family as it is, family members accept strange, compulsive, or even violent or abusive behavior as normal. They accept the unacceptable.

The people in these families are stuck in their roles and in their beliefs. Unless they get help, family members are likely to stay stuck for their entire lives, taking their roles and beliefs into adulthood and into new families.

5

When the Teenager Is the Addict

Janessa hides candy bars all over her room, even inside her shoes. She regularly skips her fifth period class to go to a nearby fast food restaurant for a second lunch. Sometimes she takes the change from her father's dresser to pay for the extra food she buys.

Curtis keeps his stash of marijuana under his mattress. He smokes pot every day, right before and right after school. He has missed basketball practice so much that he has lost his position on first string, and he is failing two subjects for the first time in his life. Curtis has learned to shoplift to get the money he needs to buy pot.

Both these teenagers are addicts.

Addiction is not the exclusive territory of adults.

Drug Use on the Rise for Teens

A survey sponsored by the National Institute of Drug Abuse in 1993 noted an increase in:

- ❑ 12th graders using any illicit drugs
- ❑ 12th graders who had used an illicit drug at least once
- ❑ 12th graders using LSD once and annually
- ❑ 8th, 10th, and 12th graders using marijuana
- ❑ 8th and 10th graders using inhalants
- ❑ 10th graders binge drinking[1]

However, addiction to drugs, alcohol, food, or a behavior poses some unique problems for teenagers and their families.

Adolescents are in the midst of the most significant physical, emotional, and cognitive changes since their first year of life. Physically they experience major growth spurts, with rapid gains in height and weight. Sex characteristics emerge during this time and include the appearance of menstrual periods and breasts in girls and voice changes and ejaculations in boys. Sometime during the teen years, both sexes develop the ability to think more abstractly. They become able to understand theory better and to envision possibilities.

Perhaps the greatest changes, however, occur in the social and emotional lives of adolescents. The teenage years are a time of preparation for adult life. Teenagers have a powerful need to develop identities as unique human beings separate from their families. They look to their peer groups as they never have before and begin to develop intense relationships away from their families. Teenagers are learning how to relate to the larger world and to figure out where they fit in that world. They are developing interests, abilities, values, and beliefs that will last a lifetime.

Adolescence is a time of learning how to function in the world outside of the family. Addiction can interrupt, delay, and even arrest healthy growth and development.[2]

Teenagers tend to take risks and try on new behaviors as part of their learning about the world. Experimenting with drugs or alcohol is a high-risk activity for teenagers (although a common one) because addiction may occur as much as five times faster in adolescents than in adults.[3]

Using drugs, smoking, overeating, bingeing and starving, and drinking alcohol are the most typical addictions among young people. Each of them has a unique impact on the physical growth and development of adolescents, but all are very similar in the way they affect the social and emotional changes of the teenage years.

Marijuana, for example, has a serious impact on the reproductive system of chronic users. Males who use marijuana regularly produce less sperm than do their nonusing peers. Marijuana appears to suppress ovulation in females who are chronic users. This fact is particularly significant for adolescents, whose reproductive systems are just developing.

Another example of the unique effect of a drug or behavior on growth and development is steroids, a class of drugs commonly abused by young athletes.

Steroids interfere with growth, weight gain, and the development of sex characteristics in adolescents who use them regularly.[4]

Eating disorders involving bingeing and starving are most common among young females. This behavior can cause loss of sex characteristics, including menstrual periods.[5]

Developmental Tasks of Adolescence

❑ Physical maturation

❑ Formal operations (the ability to think abstractly)

❑ Membership in a peer group

❑ Intimate relationships

❑ Autonomy from parents

❑ Sex role identity

❑ Internalized morality (a personal value system)

❑ Career choice

These and other drugs and behaviors, however, are very much alike in the way they interfere with social and emotional changes in an adolescent. Addictions cause problems in these areas because they inevitably interfere with the learning necessary for growth. If a teenager is thinking constantly about her weight, it is unlikely that she is exploring her future. A young person who is high on marijuana is not learning effective ways to cope with new feelings and experiences. Someone who drinks in all situations involving his or her peers is not learning the social skills necessary for getting along in the world. The intensity of the addict's relationship with his or her substance or activity leaves no room for love relationships with other people. In fact, many treatment counselors note that adolescent addicts stop maturing socially and emotionally when they become addicted. Those people who are able to get help after years of addiction often find themselves well behind their peers in maturity and accomplishment.

The families of teenage addicts have some unique problems as well. Addictive behavior, in many cases, is not drastically different from some typical adolescent behaviors, which makes it easy to deny or ignore. For example, a young woman who is obsessed with her weight is certainly not an unusual phenomenon in our society. A family truly may not notice, or may choose not to notice, the dangerous behaviors of bingeing and purging associated with this obsession. Many drugs have side effects that could appear to be typical teenage behaviors. Excessive sleeping and emotional instability, for example, are two side effects of marijuana and alcohol use that could be considered characteristic of adolescence. It was noted in Chapter 2 that the families of addicts will frequently deny or ignore the behavior of the addicted family member, and families of addicted teenagers are no exception.

The other issue facing families of teenage addicts is

A Talk With . . .

Janessa

Janessa is seventeen years old and obese. She is working with her counselor to improve her school performance and to find help for health problems related to her weight. "Food is like a friend to me. Whenever I feel bad, I eat and feel better. I know I can count on food to help me feel good. I really can't count on much else."

When Janessa was a little girl, she learned that eating changed her feelings. In her family, food is used to reward good behavior and to soothe hurt feelings. When she was small, Janessa would get ice cream after a visit to the doctor's office or a cookie to stop her tears when she hurt herself. She learned that eating helped her to forget bad feelings. Food was also used to reward good behavior and to celebrate special accomplishments in her family.

Janessa remembers a huge meal her family had in her honor when she won a coloring contest in third grade, and the treats her mother baked for Janessa and her sister in honor of good report cards. Those occasions made her feel important and valued. As she got older and was able to help herself to food, she found that she could control her feelings by eating. Eating brought back some of the good feelings of being valued and important and also seemed to help relieve her anxiety about school and her feelings of insecurity about her friendships with other kids.

Studies have shown that eating stimulates the release of endorphins, the brain chemicals responsible for mood enhancement. Endorphins are among the primary brain chemicals stimulated by the use of both alcohol and other drugs. Through her eating, Janessa was seeking a high similar to that experienced by substance abusers.[6]

As Janessa began to gain more and more weight, she began to feel guilty about eating, so she would eat more to try to get rid of the feelings of guilt. Soon she was eating all the time, trying to control how she felt.

The heavier Janessa became, the more involved her family became in trying to control her eating. They would alternately criticize, confront, threaten, and bully her, especially at mealtimes. Their constant badgering simply made Janessa crave food more. She would eat very little at the table, and she secretly binged on food she kept hidden in her room.

Not only is Janessa addicted to food, but her family is behaving like the typical family of an addict, putting all its energy into coping with the addict and with the problems caused by the addiction. They are hiding the problem from the outside world, by keeping Janessa out of sight as much as possible.

"Now my family hides food from me and never mentions eating when I am in the room. I can see them looking at me if someone outside of the family mentions food in front of me. At mealtime, I am given a plate with the food already on it. Everyone else gets to help themselves. My mother will hear about a wonderful diet one day, and the next day she has me on it. No one else in my family has a weight problem. My sister and my mom are tall and skinny. I take after the women on my dad's side. All of them have big hips and thighs. Mom thinks I just need to use self-control and exercise. She wants me to walk every night. Last fall, my parents came up with the idea that I could use the car once for every mile I walked. I know that they thought they could get me to exercise regularly that way. It didn't work, though, because I just stopped using the car.

"Mom bought me a bike two years ago, but I am too big to ride it anymore. If they would leave me alone and just let me take care of myself, I wouldn't eat so much. Even the doctor told my mother to stop trying to control what I eat. He said I would control myself when I was ready, and she couldn't change that.

"My family is embarrassed by the way I look, I just know it. We used to go out to eat or to a movie once in a while, but we don't go anywhere as a family anymore."

the need to control or fix the addictive behavior of these young people. Before children become teenagers, their parents and other adults are, for the most part, in control of their lives. In the best of situations, it is difficult for parents to step out of that role as their children begin to mature. When a teenager becomes an addict, it is not unusual for parents to step in and try to correct the young person's behavior, using the same methods they used when the teenager was much younger. The results are often the same as in the family systems of adult addicts; family members begin to take responsibility for the addict's behavior. The following stories define many of the issues facing young addicts and their families:

Curtis's Story

Curtis is fifteen years old and addicted to marijuana. His parents have been divorced for nearly three years, and Curtis regularly spends weekends and holidays at his father's apartment in a neighboring town. In the first year after the divorce, Curtis met some older boys who lived in his apartment complex. These boys smoked marijuana regularly, and Curtis joined in whenever he was there. He learned that smoking pot muted his feelings of sadness about his parents' divorce and helped him get through the good-byes that came at the end of every weekend.

One side effect of smoking marijuana is ravenous hunger. Curtis's father chuckled the first time Curtis had a hunger attack. He saw it as a sign of a growing boy. In fact, all of the early symptoms of pot smoking that Curtis exhibited were thought by his parents to be a normal part of adolescence.

Early symptoms of marijuana use may include:

- ☐ lethargy
- ☐ extreme mood swings
- ☐ forgetfulness

Also, teenagers who are involved with marijuana often exhibit that fact in the posters on their walls and on the T-shirts and jackets they wear. Their language begins to include the jargon that surrounds pot smoking.[7]

Curtis began to seek out friends at school who used marijuana so that he could smoke during the week as well as on the weekend. Subtle changes were taking place in his behavior, but his mother was involved in her own life and failed to notice what was happening. "No one noticed," Curtis explained to the treatment counselor. "My dad thought I was being a teenager, and Mom was 'in love.' All she could talk about was this new guy! I really liked using pot because I didn't have to deal with all that."

Curtis was getting deeply involved with a group of heavy pot smokers and was becoming more and more dependent on the drug to help him cope with his fears and anxieties. When he invited a girl to the movies and was turned down, he smoked pot. When he was worried about a test, he smoked pot. When he was depressed about the direction his life was going, he smoked pot.

Curtis's first failing grade did get his parents' attention. His father came in from out of town, and they both went to meet with the school counselor. She told them that teachers' reports included the information that Curtis was sleeping in class, and not turning in his homework. The counselor asked Curtis's parents if there was any possibility that Curtis was using drugs. His parents were shocked at the counselor's suggestion and strongly denied that possibility. His mother felt that Curtis was depressed, probably had never adjusted to the divorce. Both of them were sure it was a phase, but they did agree to get a tutor for Curtis for the next semester.

Curtis's grades and behavior became progressively worse over the next few months. The tutor Curtis's mother had hired finally quit, explaining that Curtis had no interest at all in his studies. Not long after that, the school suspended Curtis for shoving a teacher. Curtis's parents explained to the school counselor that they felt Curtis was being unfairly judged. He was, they believed, just a sensitive adolescent who was misunderstood by many of the adults around him. Actually, Curtis was showing some of the signs of heavy marijuana use.

Curtis's family is also behaving like a typical addict's family, denying that Curtis has a problem. If this family recognizes Curtis's drug use, they must then do something about it that will, ultimately, change their family system. They are, in effect, enabling Curtis's addiction by protecting him, as much as they can, from the consequences of his behavior. Although Curtis eventually was arrested along

Signs of Heavy Marijuana Use

- ❏ extreme hostility
- ❏ anxiety
- ❏ panic attacks
- ❏ paranoia
- ❏ loss of motivation
- ❏ hallucinations[8]

with seven other students for possession of marijuana, his parents continue to deny the problem.

Families like those of Curtis and Janessa may have some other problems to face even if their teenagers are treated successfully for their addictions. Because addiction interferes with growth and development, these young people are likely to be dependent on their families for much longer than is normally the case, while they try to catch up to their peers.

Melissa

I remember the first time I began to see my family as different from other families. It was a particularly tough time at our house. My dad had lost another job, and he and my mom were fighting every night, all night. The only sleep I got was when they stopped yelling long enough to get another drink. I stopped even trying to do my homework. My grades were dropping fast when my English teacher referred me to the counselor who asked me some questions about what was going on in my life and gave me a couple of books to read. Both the books were for children of alcoholics! I couldn't believe it! These books aren't for me, I told her. My parents are not alcoholics! She said she thought the books would be helpful anyway, so I took them.

One of the books my counselor gave me had a list of questions I could answer to see if my family really did have a problem. I only had to answer a few to realize that my parents were alcoholics. I read every word in that book, and then I read it again. I did the same thing with the other book. It was hard to believe that there were people out there that understood how I felt about myself and my life. It was almost as if the writers had lived in my family.

6

Help for Addicts' Families

———————

Like most children in the families of addicts, Melissa did not realize that her family was different. She believed that the out-of-control behaviors in her family were normal . . . that all families were like that. Because the family never talked about drinking, or the fighting and other problems caused by drinking, she was shocked to think that anyone would consider them alcoholic. The counselor knew that in order for Melissa to get help, she must first be able to admit that her family had a problem.

The children of addicts often feel very alone. Many of them suffer in silence. Melissa was fortunate to have a teacher who was concerned enough to refer her to the counselor and fortunate also, to have a counselor who had some knowledge about children of alcoholics. In fact, Melissa eventually became part of a group of students who were all children of alcoholics.

School Support Groups

Support groups are usually made up of people with similar life experiences. They are formed to offer members support and opportunities to learn how others have dealt with similar problems. Skill-building is frequently an important part of these groups. Young people who are struggling with their studies because of problems at home can learn skills that help them cope with family issues, so they can then try to improve their schoolwork.

Counselors are usually responsible for support or help groups and invite students to participate. However, it is not unusual for a counselor to start a group because students request it. The school groups may have names that conceal their purpose, to protect the privacy of the participants. Calling a group Children of Alcoholics or Children of Dysfunctional Families could lead to difficult questions and teasing from peers. Confidentiality, in fact, is a key to the success of a group. Only when students trust the process are they able to share personal experiences and feelings.

The group cannot fix a family with problems. However, young people in the families of addicts can learn in the group that they are not responsible for family problems or for fixing the problems them-selves. They may learn to take better care of their own needs instead of always being concerned with the needs of others.

Imagine that you have a parent who is under the

influence of a drug. His or her behavior is unpredictable. When using the drug, your parent may be warm, friendly, and fun to be around. As the drug wears off and he or she experiences the discomfort of withdrawal, there may be a personality change. Your parent may become angry or depressed. Unfortunately, the other family members cannot plan their lives around the drug use of one person. It is easier to ask to use the car to get to your job, for example, when your parent is high on drugs or alcohol and in a good mood. If you need the car, however, you may have to ask for it even if your parent is coming down off the drug and in an angry mood. You must constantly be on the alert, trying to get your needs met without upsetting your parent. What a comfort it would be for you to have other people to talk to who have the same problem.

Student Assistance and Peer Helper Programs

Earlier we met Tonya, a member of a suicide support group at her school. Tonya was referred to the Student Assistance Program at her school by a teacher who was concerned about her depressed behavior. The Student Assistance Program is made up of faculty and staff members at the school who work with students who are having difficulty. Tonya could have referred herself or been referred by a friend, counselor, or other adult. The team worked with Tonya to identify problem areas and to help her find solutions to her difficulties. Tonya's depression was so severe that the team contacted her father and suggested she see a doctor. Tonya was out of school and living in a psychiatric hospital for two months. When she returned to school, the Student Assistance Team once again stepped in. They suggested, among other things, her involvement in the suicide support group recently started by the counselor.

Student Assistance Teams apply the combined expertise of a variety of people to the problems any individual student is having, rather than relying on the opinion of one teacher or counselor. School nurses, teachers, coaches, administrators, psychologists, and social workers, all may be included on the team. Students are usually referred automatically if they violate the school's substance abuse policy. They must still suffer whatever consequences are required by the policy, but through the Student Assistance Team they will also be referred for treatment for substance abuse if it is determined that they need it. Counselors, administrators, and other school personnel can also refer their concerns about a student to the team.

Once a referral is received, the student's other teachers and coaches are polled to find out if this student is having problems anywhere else in school. The student's record is examined for any evidence of problems in earlier years. In high school and many middle schools, the student is asked to meet with a representative of the team to discuss the reason for the referral. At the elementary level, the parent is most often involved from the beginning. Once the problem has been clearly identified, the team works with the student toward a solution. In many cases, the parent is invited to help with the solution. Sometimes, the problem is solved without the involvement of the parent.

Student Assistance Programs, sometimes called Student Services Management Teams, are designed to help schools help students. Without these teams, teachers don't always know how to deal with many of their concerns about their students. They may know what to do about a failing grade, but not what to do about a student who is crying or sleeping in class, or is coming to school unwashed. Tonya's teacher did not have to decide whether Tonya had a serious problem or not; she simply had to refer Tonya to people better equipped to make a determination like that.

Peer Helpers are another resource for troubled students. Peer Helper Programs, available in many schools, are made up of students trained to listen to other students and refer them, when necessary, to the appropriate help. It is often easier for young people to talk to others who are their own age about their problems. Peer Helpers can offer support and friendship to students who have addicted family members. These students are trained to know how to break confidentiality when they hear of young people who are behaving in ways that may be harmful to themselves or to others.

Community Support Groups

Support and help groups can make a difference in the lives of young people. Remember Michael, from Chapter 1? His father is addicted to cocaine. In one attempt to overcome his addiction, Michael's father committed himself to a treatment center.

When someone is being treated for a chemical addiction, the family is usually involved in the treatment process. They attend therapy sessions with the addict and his psychologist or counselor and have meetings with members of other families of addicts in treatment. When the addict leaves the treatment center, he is expected to attend community meetings for addicts. Community groups are also available for these families.

Michael's dad attends meetings of Narcotics Anonymous; Michael's group is called Nar-Anon. Whether his father continues to recover from his addiction to cocaine or backslides, Michael can continue with Nar-Anon. The group offers him the same support Melissa is getting at school. It is very comforting to Michael to be with people who have shared his experience with a drug-addicted family member.

Alcoholics Anonymous (AA) is a group originally formed to help people addicted to alcohol. AA is made up of people recovering from addiction who need the support of others to help them keep sober. Alcoholics Anonymous was unique in our society when it was founded in the 1930s, because it required addicts to speak about their addiction in front of other people. At that time, America was still under the influence of the Victorian age, and people believed in keeping their problems to themselves.[1]

It wasn't until the 1960s and 1970s that it became generally accepted for people to open up and talk to each other about the most personal parts of their lives. A movement toward self-awareness developed. Rap groups formed, in which people talked openly about their feelings and shared childhood memories. As people began to share their lives, many discovered common experiences and feelings associated with having an alcoholic parent. By the early 1980s, the Adult Children of Alcoholics movement was in full swing, acknowledging hundreds of thousands of adults who were still suffering the effects of growing up in the family of someone addicted to alcohol.

Help For Families

Al-Anon is a support group for families of alcoholics, founded by the wives of early AA members. It was this group that first gave recognition to the suffering of the families of addicts. Children in alcoholic families attended Al-Anon if they wanted help. Then, in the 1950s, Alateen was started by a high school student in California who wanted to talk to other teenagers with alcoholic parents.[2]

Experts suggest that one in four Americans has been affected by an alcohol problem of a family member. From the Adult Children of Alcoholics movement, it was a short step to identifying the problems of families of drug addicts. The President's Commission on Model State Drug Laws, 1993 Executive Summary, directly addresses the needs of the children in these families by stating: "Student assistance programs (in public schools) will be expanded. Children of alcoholics and (drug) addicts will be allowed to pursue needed counseling to cope with and address their parents' addictions." It was another short step for society to begin to recognize the impact of other unhealthy behaviors on families. Gambling, eating disorders, and relationships/sex are among the behaviors first recognized as addictive. Now there are groups for many kinds of addiction and support for family members with a variety of needs. Many of these groups follow the model of Alcoholics Anonymous.

Mental Health Centers

Earlier in the book we met Leonard, whose father is addicted to gambling. Leonard talked to his counselor about some of his family's problems. The counselor felt that he could benefit from more help than she was able to offer in school. At her suggestion, and with the support of his mother, Leonard began to see a psychologist at the local mental health center. If the psychologist thought Leonard needed medication, she could refer him to a psychiatrist. After working with the psychologist for a while, Leonard began to understand that he was not responsible for fixing his family. He learned that he could pay attention to his own needs without hurting his mother or his brothers and sisters.

When Leonard stopped to see his counselor after attending several months of sessions at the mental health center, he told her he had given up one of his jobs and had joined a community softball team. He mentioned that his mother was glad he was playing softball, but very upset about the loss of income from his second job. In fact, Leonard said, the family had been in an uproar since he made those two decisions. His mother, of course, wanted what was best for her son and agreed to his seeing a psychologist. Like most people, she didn't understand the impact that a change in one family member has on the entire family.

Leonard upset the family system by giving up his second job and signing up for softball. He was no longer contributing as much needed money as before to support his family and to cover his father's gambling addiction, and he would not be as available to help his mother as he had been. His mother and his brothers and sisters had become used to the role Leonard played in the family, and they were upset by the changes. The reaction of his family could make it hard for Leonard to continue to change and grow. It would be better for him and for the rest of the family to be working on the problems in the family together.

Teenage Addicts

What happens when the teenager in the family is the addict? Janessa, the food-addicted teenager discussed in the previous chapter, has been receiving the assistance of her counselor for some of her problems. The counselor has referred her to an eating disorder clinic, where she can get medical treatment for her obesity and counseling for her addictive behavior. An important part of Janessa's treatment will involve her family. They have been resistant to meeting with anyone, expressing the feeling that this is Janessa's problem, not theirs.

Curtis, whose family denies that he has a serious problem, is in treatment at the insistence of the court. Thus far, his family has been unwilling to cooperate with Curtis's treatment, insisting that he is not being treated fairly. His parents insist that treatment is a drastic and unnecessary step.

Several special problems face an addicted teenager. The addiction may interfere with academic performance, as it did in the cases of both Curtis and Janessa. Drugs are notorious for affecting the success of young people in school, but gambling, unhealthy relationships, and other addictions can also have a serious impact.

Even more than adults, teenagers need the support of their families to overcome their addictions successfully. They are more dependent on others for what they do, how they do it, where they go, how they get there, what they eat or do not eat. If they are to succeed in their efforts to change, the family must be prepared to accept that change. If Janessa wishes to change her eating habits, her family must learn to give up trying to control her. They must be able to stand back and allow her the freedom to change in her own way.

Medical Help

For food, alcohol, and drug addictions, there is often the need to involve doctors to treat the physical problems that accompany such addictions. However, when food or substances are abused, the physical and the psychological aspects of the addiction must both be treated. The impact of drugs on the developing body of the teenager was discussed in the previous chapter. Food addiction has its own set of physical complications, which can put young people at great risk for numerous health problems that can lead to early death.

All teenagers who become addicted—whether to substances, food, or activities—are delayed in their maturity. They stop learning when they start drinking, gambling, overeating, or using drugs and only begin learning again when they stop. While most teenagers are developing their own identities, learning about themselves as separate and unique individuals, addicted young people identify only with their addictions and with the people who share their addictions.

While other young people are thinking about their futures, addicted teenagers are thinking about their addictions—when they will be able to do the activity again or how they will get more of their drug. While other young people are learning about healthy relationships, addicted teenagers are having an unhealthy relationship with an activity or a substance.

Janessa said earlier, "Food is like a friend to me. Whenever I feel bad, I eat and feel better. I know I can count on food to help me feel good. I really can't count on much else." Because Janessa is counting on food to keep her happy, she does not reach out or try to make friends. Even if Janessa's treatment is successful, and she is able to control her eating and to lose weight, she will be less mature than her nonaddicted peers and may still have some difficulty with relationships.

Kim, whose scapegoat role in her family was discussed in an earlier chapter, is more likely to get help than some of the other young people in this book. She is the student who is causing problems for the school, and she may get in trouble with the law. When that happens, she will receive help through numerous intervention programs available through the schools and the criminal justice system. Her difficulties are the most obvious, and so they will get the most attention. If the scapegoat is more likely to get help, her family is more likely to be helped as well.

Help for Families

Help is available to the families of addicts in many and varied forms. There are self-help books for children and older family members, as well as books that

Help Yourself First

If someone in your family is an addict, there are some things you can do to help yourself:

- Talk about your feelings with a close friend, relative, or caring adult. It is perfectly normal to share your feelings, and talking can help you feel less lonely.

- Get involved in activities that you enjoy. You will get a break from the problems at home, and you will feel better about yourself.

- Attend an Alateen meeting, or find a support group of other teens who will be able to relate to what you are going through. You are not alone.

- Don't try to change the addicted person in your family. Just as you are not responsible for his or her addiction, you are not responsible for fixing the problem.

- Practice having fun. Sometimes things can be so stressful at home that it is even hard to find something to smile about. Make an effort to find entertaining things to do and to laugh about.

- Treat yourself now and then. Take care of you.

explain and offer help for various kinds of addiction. Most communities have anonymous groups not only for addicts, but for family members as well. Schools usually have some form of Student Assistance Team available. Treatment for addiction is available through community mental health centers and family services as well as through private hospitals.

Chapter Notes

Chapter 1

1. Marilyn A. Jensen, "School Programming for the Prevention of Addictions," *The School Counselor*, January 1992, vol. 39, pp. 202–210.

2. John Edwards, Ph.D., *Working with Families, Guidelines and Techniques* (Durham, N.C.: 1993).

3. Institute For Health Policy, Brandeis University, *Substance Abuse: The Nation's Number One Health Problem, Key Indicators for Policy* (Princeton, N.J.: Robert Wood Johnson Foundation, 1993), from 1994 National Household Survey by Substance Abuse and Mental Health Services Administration.

4. Ibid., p. 34.

5. Susan Giarratano, Ed.D., and Dale Evans, Hs.D., *Entering Adulthood: A Curriculum for Grades 9–12* (Santa Cruz, Calif.: Network Publications, 1995), p. 85.

6. Robert L. DuPont, Jr., M.D., *Getting Tough on Gateway Drugs: A Guide for the Family* (Washington, D.C.: American Psychiatric Press, Inc., 1984), p. 27.

7. Institute for Health Policy, p. 31.

8. Southeast Regional Center for Drug Free Schools and Communities, *Fostering Resiliency in Kids: Protective Factors in the Family and Community* (Louisville, Ky.: University of Louisville, 1991), pp. 2–4.

9. Ibid., p. 2.

10. *Fostering Resiliency in Kids: Protective Factors in the Family, School and Community*, Western Center for Drug Free Schools and Communities, Portland, Ore., August 1991, pp. 2, 12.

11. John Bradshaw, *Bradshaw On: The Family—A Revolutionary Way of Self Discovery* (Deerfield Beach, Fla.: Health Communications, 1988) pp. 39–40.

Chapter 2

1. Nicholas Zill and Christine Winquist Nord, *Running In Place—How American Families are Faring in a Changing Economy and An Industrialistic Society* (Washington, D.C.: Child Trends Inc., 1994), p. 6.

2. Miriam McLaughlin and Sandra Hazouri, *TLC-Tutoring, Leading, Cooperating: Training Activities for Elementary School Students* (Minneapolis: Educational Media, 1992), p. 22.

3. John Bradshaw, *Bradshaw On: The Family—A Revolutionary Way of Self-Discovery* (Deerfield Beach, Fla.: Health Communications, 1988).

4. Rudolf Dreikurs, M.D., with Vicki Soltz, R.N., *Children: The Challenge* (New York: E. P. Dutton, 1987), p. 6.

5. Murray Dubin, "Sex Addiction, Out of the Closet," Knight-Ridder News Service, *Raleigh News and Observer,* April 30, 1995, p. 6E.

6. David Shipman, *Judy Garland: The Secret Life of an American Legend* (New York: Hyperion, 1993), p. 378.

Chapter 3

1. Laurence Leamer, *The Kennedy Women: The Saga of an American Family* (New York: Villard Books, 1994), p. 435.

2. Mark Gold, M.D., *The Facts About Adolescent Drug Abuse* (New York: Bantam Books, 1992), p. 6.

3. Robert L. DuPont, Jr., M.D., *Getting Tough on Gateway Drugs: A Guide for the Family* (Washington, D.C.: American Psychiatric Press, Inc., 1984), p. 19.

4. Jenson, pp. 203–205.

5. Institute for Health Policy, Brandeis University, *Substance Abuse: The Nation's Number One Health Problem, Key Indicators for Policy* (Princeton, N.J.: Robert Wood Johnson Foundation, 1993), p. 22.

6. Myra Vanderpool Gormley, *Family Diseases—Are You at Risk?* (Baltimore, Md.: Genealogical Publishing Co., Inc., 1989), p. 59.

7. *Florida's Challenge: A Guide to Educating Substance-Exposed Children*, Florida Department of Education, Substance-Exposed Children's Project, Tallahassee, Fla., 1990.

8. Diana Kronstadt, "Complex Developmental Issues of Pre-Natal Drug Exposure," *The Future of Children*, Spring 1991, pp. 46–48.

9. Ibid., pp. 39–40.

10. Dennis C. Daley, *Kicking Addictive Habits Once and For All* (Lexington, Mass.: D. C. Heath and Company, 1991), pp. 101–103.

11. Jon Zonderman and Laura Shader, M.D., *The Encyclopedia of Psychoactive Drugs, Series 2: Drugs and Disease* (New York: Chelsea House Publishers, 1987), p. 65.

12. Institute for Health Policy, p. 7.

13. Art Schlichter and Judith Valente, "A Long Road to Daylight," *People Weekly*, January 15, 1996, pp. 81–87.

Chapter 4

1. Gaynelle Whitlock, Ed.D., *How Schools Can Help Children of Alcoholics* (Richmond, Va.: School of Education, Virginia Commonwealth University, 1991), pp. 18–26.

2. John Bradshaw, *Bradshaw On: The Family—A Revolutionary Way of Self-Discovery* (Deerfield Beach, Fla.: Health Communications, 1988), p. 77.

3. Whitlock, pp. 21–24.

4. Ibid.

5. Ibid.

6. Claudia Black, Ph.D., MSW, *It Will Never Happen to Me* (Denver, Colo.: M.A.C. Printing and Publications Division, 1981), pp. 53–64.

7. Whitlock, pp. 18–26.

8. Ibid., pp. 34–41.

9. Ibid., pp. 21–24.

Chapter 5

1. *Center Page*, U.S. Department of Education, vol. 3, Summer 1994, p. 1.

2. Gayle Dorman et al., *Living with 10–15-Year-Olds: A Parent Education Curriculum* (Carrboro, N.C.: Center for Early Adolescence, University of North Carolina-Chapel Hill, 1986), pp. IV, 16–17.

3. Mark Gold, M.D., *The Facts About Adolescent Drug Abuse* (New York: Bantam Books, 1992), p. 9.

4. William H. Masters, M.D., Virginia E. Johnson, and Robert C. Kolodny, M.D., *Heterosexuality* (New York: HarperCollins, 1994), p. 353.

5. Ibid., p. 348.

6. Julia Ross, M.A., "Food Addiction: A New Look at the Nature of Craving," *Addiction and Recovery*, vol. 13, no. 5., September/October 1993, p. 18.

7. *Marijuana: A Second Look at a Drug of Isolation* (Daly City, Calif.: Krames Communication, 1988), pp. 3–7.

8. Ibid., pp. 11–12.

Chapter 6

1. *Al-Anon's Twelve Steps & Twelve Traditions* (New York: Al-Anon Family Group Headquarters, Inc., 1988), pp. xi–xii.

2. Ibid.

Further Reading

Ackerman, Robert J., ed. *Growing in the Shadow: Children of Alcoholics.* Pompano Beach, Fla.: Health Communications, Inc., 1986.

Al-Anon's *Twelve Steps and Twelve Traditions.* New York: Al-Anon Family Group Headquarters, Inc., 1988.

Boller, Jr., Paul F. *Presidential Wives: An Anecdotal History.* New York: Oxford Press, 1988.

Daley, Dennis C. *Kicking Addictive Habits Once and for All.* Lexington, Mass.: D. C. Heath and Company, 1991.

Dorman, Gayle, et al. *Living with 10–15-year-olds: A Parent Education Curriculum.* Carrboro, N.C.: Center for Early Adolescence, UNC-CH, 1986.

Dreikurs, Rudolf, M.D., with Vicki Solty, R.N. *Children: The Challenge.* New York: E. P. Dutton, 1987.

Dubin, Murray. "Sex Addiction Out of the Closet." *News and Observer*, Knight-Ridder Publications, Raleigh, N.C. (April 30, 1995), 6E.

Dupont, Robert L., Jr. *Getting Tough on Gateway Drugs: A Guide for the Family.* Washington, D.C.: American Psychiatric Press, Inc., 1984.

Edwards, John, Ph.D. *Working with Families: Guidelines and Techniques.* Durham, N.C., 1993, (self-published).

Fischer, Carolyn A., and Carol A. Schwartz, eds. *Encyclopedia of Associations 1996, 30th Edition.* New York: Gale Research, Inc., 1995.

Florida's Challenge: A Guide to Educating Substance Exposed Children. Tallahassee, Fla.: Florida Department of Education, 1991.

Foster, Sharon. "Teenage Addiction of the 90's: Compulsive Gambling." *Counseling Today*, American Counseling Association, June 1995.

Giarratano, Susan, Ed.D., and Dale Evans, Hs.D. *Entering Adulthood: A Curriculum for Grades 9–12.* Santa Cruz, Calif.: Network Publications, 1995.

Gold, Mark, M.D. *The Facts About Adolescent Drug Abuse.* New York: Bantam Books, 1992.

Gormley, Myra Vanderpool. *Family Diseases—Are You at Risk?* Baltimore, Md.: Genealogical Publishing Co., Inc., 1989.

Institute For Health Policy, Brandeis University, Robert Wood Johnson Foundation. *Substance Abuse: The Nation's Number One Health Problem*, Key Indicators for Policy. Princeton, N.J.: 1993.

Jensen, Marilyn A. "School Programming for the Prevention of Addictions." *The School Counselor*, vol. 39, January 1992, 202–209.

Kronstady, Diana. "Complex Developmental Issues of Pre-natal Drug Exposure." *The Future of Children*, Spring 1991, 36–49.

Leamer, Laurence. *The Kennedy Women.* New York: Ivy Books, 1994.

Masters, William H., M.D., Virginia E. Johnson, and Robert C. Kolodny, M.D. *Heterosexuality.* New York: HarperCollins, 1994.

McLaughlin, Miriam, and Sandra Hazouri. *TLC— Tutoring, Leading, Cooperating: Training Activities for Elementary School Students.* Minneapolis: Educational Media, 1992.

Mooney, Al J., M.D., Arlene Eisenberg, and Howard Eisenberg. *The Recovery Book.* New York: Workman Publishing, 1992.

Ross, Julia, M.A. "Food Addiction: A New Look at the Nature of Craving." *Addiction and Recovery,* vol. 13, September/October 1993, 17–19.

Rudgley, Richard. *Essential Substances: A Cultural History of Intoxicants in Society.* New York: Kodansha International, 1994.

Schlichter, Art. "A Long Road to Daylight." *People Magazine,* January 15, 1996, 81–87.

Shipman, David. *Judy Garland: The Secret Life of an American Legend.* New York: Hyperion, 1992.

Southeast Regional Center for Drug Free Schools and Communities. *Fostering Resiliency in Kids: Protective Factors in the Family and Community.* Louisville, Ky.: University of Louisville, 1991.

Swisher, Karin L., ed. *Drug Abuse: Opposing Viewpoints.* San Diego, Calif.: Greenhaven Press, 1994.

Whitlock, Gaynelle, Ed.D. *How Schools Can Help Children of Alcoholics.* Richmond, Va.: School of Education, Virginia Commonwealth University, 1991.

Wills, Christopher. *Exons, Introns, and Talking Genes: The Science Behind the Human Genome Project.* New York: HarperCollins, 1991.

Yates, Alayne, M.D. *Compulsive Exercise and the Eating Disorders: Toward an Integrated Theory of Activity.* New York: Brimmer/Mazel Publishers, 1991.

Zonderman, Jon, and Laura Shader, M.D. *The Encyclopedia of Psychoactive Drugs, Series 2: Drugs and Disease.* New York: Chelsea House Publishers, 1987.

Answer Key

1. **False.** Anyone close to the addict is affected by his or her behavior.
2. **False.** Addicted families often hide their problems even from close family friends.
3. **False.** As many as one in four schoolchildren is affected by alcohol addiction alone.
4. **True.** Healthy families argue and are able to resolve their conflicts.
5. **False.** Children have no control over a parent's addiction.
6. **True.** Research has identified a gene for alcoholism in some males. Children also learn addictive behavior from the adults in their lives.
7. **True.** However, the majority of the research on addiction focuses on substance abuse.
8. **True.** Teenagers from families in which someone is an addict may not have learned how to relate to others in healthy ways.
9. **True.** Most people who drink are not alcoholic.
10. **True.** Addiction interferes with normal growth and development in adolescents.
11. **True.** Support groups exist for dealing with many of the problems caused by addiction.
12. **True.** Schools sometimes have their own chapters of Alateen.

Index